THE NOTEBOOK OF DOOM

SNEEZE OF THE OCTO-SCHNOZZ

by Troy Cummings

BRANCHES™
SCHOLASTIC INC.

TABLE OF CONTENTS

To Ben and Claire, who rock.

Thank you, Katie Carella and Liz Frances. We made it all the way to book eleven before making a booger joke. A WORLD RECORD!

Library of Congress Cataloging-in-Publication Data

Names: Cummings, Troy, author. | Cummings, Troy. Notebook of doom; 11.Title: Sneeze of the octo-schnozz / by Troy Cummings. Description: New York, NY: Branches/Scholastic Inc., [2017] | Series: The Notebook of Doom ; 11 | Summary: Since the Notebook of Doom was stolen Alexander and the other monster hunters of Stermont Elementary have been operating without its assistance and now they are confronted by a large and stinky monster with eight powerful noses that can deliver a slimy sneeze with the power of a cannon — and somehow they must figure out its weakness. Identifiers: LCCN 2016030466|

Subjects: LCSH: Monsters — Juvenile fiction. | Elementary schools — Juvenile fiction. | Friendship — Juvenile fiction. | Horror tales. | CVAC: Horror stories. | Monsters — Fiction. | Schools — Fiction. | Friendship — Fiction. | LCGFT: Horror fiction.
Classification: LCC PZ7.C91494 Sn 2017 | DDC 813.6 [Fic] — dc23 LC record available at https://lccn.loc.gov/2016030466

ISBN-13: 978-93-8631-384-3

Book design by Liz Frances

First edition, January 2017

This edition, September 2019

Printed at Shivam Offset Press, New Delhi

CHAPTER 1

A CLOSE-KNIT GROUP

"Wait up, Dottie!" Alexander shouted.

He jogged to catch up with his friend as she skipped along the forest path.

"No way!" Dottie called back. "I love S.S.M.P. meetings!"

S.S.M.P. stood for Super Secret Monster Patrol, a group of kids sworn to protect the town of Stermont from monsters. Alexander was the group's leader. Dottie was its newest member.

They soon came upon an old caboose, covered with vines.

"Gosh," said Alexander. "Our headquarters is overgrown."

"At least the flowers smell good!" Dottie said, sniffing the air. "Oh — what's this?"

There was some red yarn tangled in the vines. The yarn wiggled.

"Someone's pulling the other end!" Dottie said.

She followed the yarn, which looped around the caboose and under the back door. Dottie opened the door. Alexander followed her inside.

RARRR!!!

A two-headed creature leaped out from behind a table.

"MONSTER!" Dottie cried, jumping back.

"Watch out! It's a knit-wit!" said Alexander.

CLACKITY-CLICK! The monster wiggled its claws.

"How do we stop it, Salamander?" asked Dottie.

Salamander was Alexander's nickname. His friends called him that at home, at school, or when they were under attack by a two-headed yarn creature.

"Quick! We need to unravel it!" said Alexander.

Dottie leaped toward the monster and grabbed a big fistful of yarn. She yanked hard. The monster spun around, crashing into a shelf.

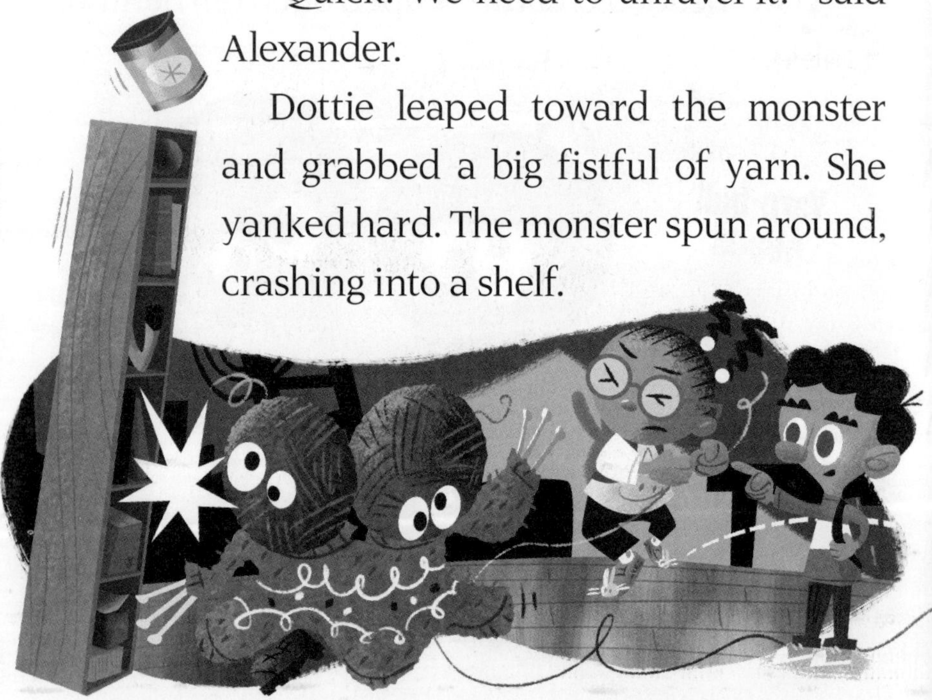

CLONK! An old tin coffee can fell to the floor. Something fuzzy rolled out.

A horrible smell filled the caboose.

"Time out!" said one of the monster's heads. **POP! POP!** The knit-wit pulled off its yarn-ball heads. Inside were the other two members of the S.S.M.P.

Nikki pulled out a stopwatch. "Forty-seven seconds!" she said. "A new record!"

"What just happened?" asked Dottie, holding her nose from the stench.

"That was an S.S.M.P. monster-fighting test," said Alexander. "You did awesome!"

Dottie grinned.

Alexander's eyes watered from the smell of the stinky fuzzy thing.

"What was in that old can, anyhow?" he asked, opening a window.

Rip read the label on the can.

"Funky cheese," he said. "Why would the old S.S.M.P. keep —"

HOO-RONNNNNK!!!

A loud honking sound rattled the windows.

The four monster-fighters gasped.

"Is this part of the test?" asked Dottie.

"No," said Alexander. "That sounded like a moose."

"Or a foghorn," said Nikki.

"Or a burping bullfrog," said Rip.

Something rammed into the caboose. Junk fell off the walls. Alexander, Rip, Nikki, and Dottie fell into a tumble of yarn and funky cheese.

A pointy gray horn punched through the wall, then ripped back out, leaving a huge hole.

"What was that?" asked Dottie.

"It looked like a rhino horn!" said Nikki.

Alexander heard a snuffling sound, then a sharp intake of breath.

WHA-CHOOEY!!!

A gust of wind blasted through the hole, sending papers flying.

PUMM-PUMM-PUMM! The S.S.M.P. heard heavy footsteps running into the woods, and then: silence.

CHAPTER 2 SLIME TIME

Is the monster gone?” asked Dottie.

Rip stuck his head through the giant hole in the wall. “No sign of it!” he said.

“Come on,” said Alexander. “Let’s see how bad this looks from the outside.”

“I’ll use our new emergency exit!” said Rip. He jumped through the hole, hitting the ground with a **SPLAT!**

Alexander, Nikki, and Dottie used the door.

“Are you all right, Rip?” asked Alexander.

Nikki started laughing. Rip was lying in a pool of drippy green slime.

"Join me for a swim?" he asked.

"Bleccch!" said Dottie. "Slime is everywhere! And it ruined the flowers!"

"The monster with the horn must have made this mess, right?" asked Nikki.

"Yes," said Alexander, quickly unzipping his backpack. He paused. And then re-zipped it. "Crud! I keep forgetting the notebook was stolen!"

"Stolen by our teacher," added Dottie.

"Dr. Tallow was no teacher!" said Rip. "She was an evil, shape-shifting blob!"

"Yeah, and she gave our notebook to the boss-monster," said Nikki.

Alexander sighed. On his first day in Stermont, he had uncovered an old notebook full of monster facts. It had helped the S.S.M.P. defeat tons of monsters — but now it was gone.

"We've got to get the notebook back," said Alexander.

"How?" said Rip. "We don't know who the boss-monster is."

Dottie gasped. "Could the boss-monster be the thing that just rammed our headquarters!?"

"Maybe," said Alexander. "Let's write down what we know about this caboose-crasher."

Alexander scribbled some notes on a scrap of paper.

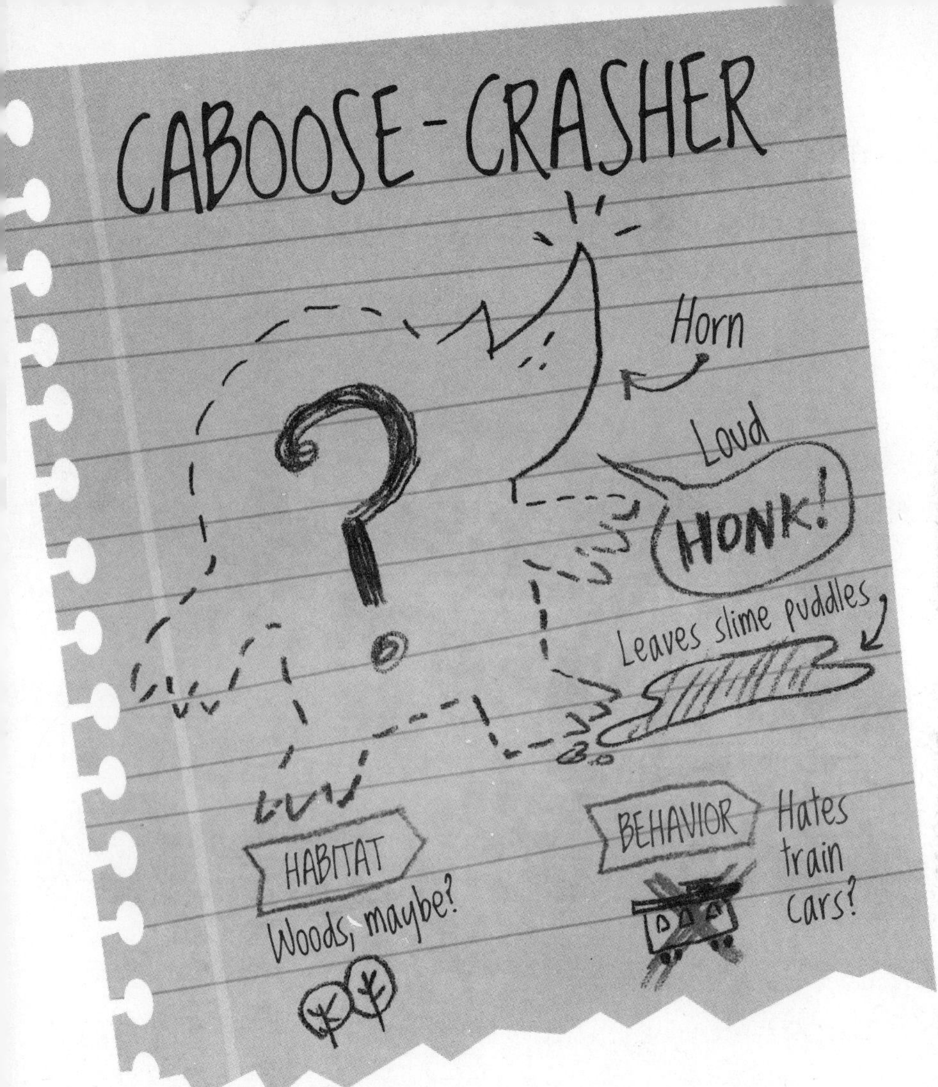

"Not much to go on, is it?" said Nikki.

Rip flung slime at Alexander. "Sounds like this meeting is over," he said. "Let's break for dinner."

"Wait! I almost forgot," said Dottie, opening her bunny backpack. "You're invited to my birthday party!" She handed out colorful envelopes.

"Thanks!" said Alexander.

"Pirates?" said Rip. "ARRRR-some!"

"Can't wait, Dottie!" said Nikki. "See you guys tomorrow!"

CHAPTER 3 SUNDAY MAIL

"Peeeee-yew!" said Alexander's dad. "What's that dog-awful smell?"

Alexander had just walked into the kitchen. He sniffed his shirt.

"Um, funky cheese?" said Alexander.

"Why don't you go take a bath and un-funky yourself while I finish dinner," said his dad.

Alexander tromped upstairs. Fifteen minutes later, he tromped back down, in pajamas.

"Ah! Squeaky clean!" his dad said. "And here's your bathrobe — fresh from the dryer!"

"Thanks, Dad," said Alexander, slipping into the robe. It felt soft and warm, but smelled flowery. "My robe smells like a rose garden."

"I may have overdone it on the fabric softener," said his dad. "But it beats stinky cheese!"

"Speaking of cheese — let's eat!" said Alexander, taking a seat.

His dad scooped lasagna onto Alexander's plate. "Oh, you got mail today," he said.

"On a Sunday?" asked Alexander.

"Yeah," said his dad. "It must have been hand-delivered."

He handed Alexander an envelope.

Alexander frowned as he opened it.

STERMONT
ELEMENTARY
OFFICE OF THE PRINCIPAL

Alexander:

Your teacher, Dr. Tallow, no longer works at Stermont Elementary.

That's no surprise! As Alexander chewed his lasagna, he thought of Dr. Tallow melting into a goop-blob, attacking the S.S.M.P., and then hardening into a spiky statue.

Therefore, her students have been moved into other classrooms. You, Alexander, will now report to my office on the thirteenth floor for one-on-one lessons.

Until tomorrow,

Principal Vanderpants

Alexander dropped his fork.

"You are so lucky, Al!" said Alexander's dad, reading over his shoulder. "Just think — private lessons with your principal."

Class without my friends?! thought Alexander. *I'd rather be trampled by a caboose-crasher!*

CHAPTER 4

THE UPSTAIRS BASEMENT

Since moving to Stermont, Alexander had been swallowed by a fish-monster, squished by a bubble-wrap mummy, and zapped by electric bugs. He'd survived each attack for two reasons:

1. He had the notebook.
2. His friends were by his side.

Now, neither of these things was true. And to top it all off, his new teacher was the strictest, most serious person he'd ever known.

Alexander dragged himself into the shiny, towering lobby of his school. His shoulders slumped on the long escalator ride to the thirteenth floor.

Alexander had been all over his new school, but this was his first trip to the principal's office. *First of many*, he thought.

He plodded down the hallway, pausing at a large, stone door. Everything in this school was shiny and high-tech, except for this door.

Alexander cupped his ear to the cold stone.

SCRITCHHH! A faint scraping sound came from the door.

"Alexander!"

Alexander jumped. He turned to see Principal Vanderpants standing nearby, arms folded.

"This way, Alexander." Ms. Vanderpants led him down the hall to her office. Everything in the room was clean and gray. Except for a large white bucket near the door.

Didn't Nikki say something about a bucket when she got in trouble last week? Alexander thought.

"Have a seat," said Ms. Vanderpants. "I expect you to work hard, even when I am dealing with principal matters. Any questions?"

"Um," said Alexander. "Why does our school have a 'basement' on the thirteenth floor?"

Ms. Vanderpants narrowed her eyes. "It's a . . . storage room," she said. "Now, shall we get to work?"

She handed Alexander a spelling worksheet.

Alexander started writing. The room was silent except for his scratching pencil.

At one point, the phone rang.

"Ms. Vanderpants," said Ms. Vanderpants.

Alexander listened while he worked.

"I'm not surprised the milk went bad. That cooler has been overheating since our electricity problem a while back," said Ms. Vanderpants. "What?! Someone *stole* the spoiled milk? Well, clean up the mess and —"

The call was interrupted by a terrible noise blaring through the window.

Alexander gasped. *The honk of the caboose-crasher!*

Ms. Vanderpants looked at Alexander. Then she slammed the phone down. "I'll be right back." She marched out of the room.

Did Ms. Vanderpants hear the monster, too? Alexander wondered. *I wish lunch would get here — I've got to tell my friends the caboose-crasher is back!*

CHAPTER 5

TOTALLY UNCOOL

The lunch line was empty by the time Alexander got to the cafeteria. He read the menu as he grabbed his tray.

Alexander smelled a sharp, stinky odor.

Ugh! What are they putting in those PBJs? he thought as he reached into the milk cooler.

But instead of a milk carton, he had grabbed an ear.

"Eep!" A frightened janitor stood up.

"Mr. Hoarsely!" said Alexander.

Besides being the janitor, Mr. Hoarsely was the school nurse, secretary, gym coach, and bus driver. He was also a former S.S.M.P. member. And he seemed to be the only grown-up who could see monsters.

"Oh! Alexander," said Mr. Hoarsely. He was holding a damp sponge. "I thought the m-m-m-monster had come back!"

"Monster?" asked Alexander.

"The monster who did *this*!" whispered Mr. Hoarsely. He pointed to a gash on the cooler. "Late last night, something tore into this cooler and stole all the spoiled milk — nine hundred eighty-four cartons!"

Alexander frowned, thinking of the hole in the caboose. But that hole was roundish. This gash was jagged. *It's like the thief used a giant can opener,* thought Alexander.

"The milk-thief sloshed sour milk all over the place!" Mr. Hoarsely continued. "And this smell is impossible to scrub out!"

"Yeesh," said Alexander. "Good luck."

He left the lunch line and found his friends at a table.

"Salamander!" said Rip. "Welcome to the stink-a-teria!"

"Guess what, guys!" said Alexander. "I heard the caboose-crasher's honk again!"

"Us, too!" said Dottie. "Earlier this morning."

"Did you *see* the monster, Salamander?" asked Nikki. "Is that why you're late?"

"No," said Alexander. "My new teacher kept me past the bell."

"Yikes," Rip said, taking a bite of his sandwich. "So who'd you get?"

"Principal Vanderpants," said Alexander.

PPPPBTHTHH! Rip sprayed PBJ all over the table. "*Vanderpants!?*" he said.

"Yup — just her and me," said Alexander. "Who did you guys get?"

"I'm in Mrs. Clambert's class," said Dottie.

"Rip and I got Mrs. Felix," said Nikki.

"So," said Rip. "What's Vanderpants like as a teacher?"

"Strict," said Alexander. "And strange. She has this white bucket . . ." He turned to Nikki. "Didn't you see it in her office before?"

"Yeah," said Nikki. "She kept lugging it around last Friday. Pretty wacko."

"Alright — enough about our principal," said Dottie, grinning. "Look what I brought!"

She took a pink cupcake from her lunchbox. "My party's not until tomorrow, but I thought we could sneak a taste!"

She divided the cupcake into quarters.

Three seconds later, it was gone.

“Mmm!” said Nikki. “Strawberry’s my favorite!”

“Yum!” said Rip, brushing a crumb from his cheek. “Too bad we can’t, uh —” He paused, and began scratching his ears.

“Are you all right, Rip?” Alexander asked.

“My ears are itching like crazy!” he said. He scratched faster.

“Are you allergic to strawberries?” asked Nikki.

“No way! I eat them all the time,” said Rip. “Are my ears red?”

Dottie took a look. “Uh,” she said. “They’re actually turning . . . blue!”

Alexander stood up. “Come on, Rip. Let’s get Nurse Hoarsely.”

“Fine, Salamander,” said Rip. “Just don’t let me miss recess — I have a perfect attendance record!”

CHAPTER 6

DISCONNECT THE DOTS

"Ugh!" Rip groaned. "It feels like I'm wearing cactus earmuffs!"

"Just keep moving!" said Alexander. He herded Rip toward the broken cooler.

Alexander did a double take.

"What is it?" said Rip. "Are my ears blue-er?" He looked at his reflection in a spoon. Now his face was covered in blue spots!

"What is happening to me?!" Rip yelled. "And where is Hoarsely?!"

Mr. Hoarsely popped up, holding his smelly sponge. "Here I am!" He saw Rip's polka-dotted face and yelped, squeezing stinky water onto the floor.

"Come with me!" he said.

The three of them rushed to the nurse's office.

Mr. Hoarsely tossed the sponge in a corner, washed his hands, and put on a stethoscope.

"Okay," said Mr. Hoarsely at last. "I'm no doctor, but —" He paused. He and Alexander were both staring at Rip, wide-eyed.

"What now?!" said Rip.

"Uh," said Mr. Hoarsely. "Those blue spots are gone."

"And your ears are both back to normal," said Alexander.

"Hello, handsome!" said Rip, smiling at himself in the mirror. "But — what happened?"

Mr. Hoarsely frowned. "I'm not sure. Are you allergic to anything?"

"No," said Rip.

Mr. Hoarsely pulled out a medical book. "Let's see . . . Blue spots? . . . Aquamarine bumps? . . . Navy freckles?" He closed the book. "Nothing!"

HOO-RONNNNNK!!!

BLAM! The door slammed shut.

"Eep!" Mr. Hoarsely dove under the cot. He looked toward the door. "Wh-wh-where did my sponge go?"

Alexander ran to the door. The stinky sponge was gone.

"Yechh!" said Rip. "Who would steal a grody old sponge?"

Then the bell rang.

CHAPTER

7 ROTTEN EGGS

That afternoon, Alexander did his math, science, and reading with no bathroom breaks. Ms. Vanderpants didn't let him leave until twenty minutes after the final bell.

"Good enough for your first day, Alexander," said Ms. Vanderpants. "You may leave."

Rip and Nikki were waiting for Alexander in the lobby.

"Sorry I'm late," said Alexander.

"Poor Salamander," said Nikki. "Principal Vanderpants is really working you."

The three friends walked a few blocks in silence — until Rip whooped with joy.

"A garbage truck!" he shouted, pointing down the street. "Let's go watch it crush stuff!"

They made their way to the truck, which was surprisingly clean. And totally empty. The trash collector was scratching her head.

"Shoot!" said Rip. "There's no trash to smash!"

"You're telling me!" said the trash collector. "Every can on this route was empty. Somebody must have dumped them before I came along!"

Alexander raised an eyebrow. It stayed raised for the rest of the walk home.

"A clean garbage truck?" he said. "Empty trash cans? Something stinks about all this!"

"You mean something *doesn't* stink," said Rip.

Alexander rolled his eyes. "Guys, watch out for caboose-crashers. I'll see you tomorrow."

He cut across his yard.

SLAM! His dad burst onto the front porch. He held a yellow bowl in one hand, and his nose with the other.

“Stand back, Al!” he shouted. He raced to the trash can, tossed the bowl inside, and slammed the lid shut.

“What’s so stinky, Dad?” asked Alexander.

“My homemade tuna salad,” Alexander’s dad said, wiping his brow. “The eggs had gone bad. Also the tuna . . . The mayo, too, now that I think of it.” He patted his son’s head. “So we’re ordering pizza!”

“This reminds me of last week’s meatball disaster,” mumbled Alexander.

“Yeah, yeah. Hey, I’ll race you to the door!” said his dad. “Last one there is a — uh, never mind.”

Alexander headed inside and flopped down on the couch. His nose wrinkled. The whole house smelled like rotten tuna salad.

What a stinky day! he thought. *My one-on-one class stinks. Rip's blue spots stink! The tuna salad* really *stinks . . .*

He quickly sat up.

The milk cooler was stinky, too . . . and the funky cheese yesterday . . . Could the caboose-crasher be connected to stinky stuff?

He made some notes.

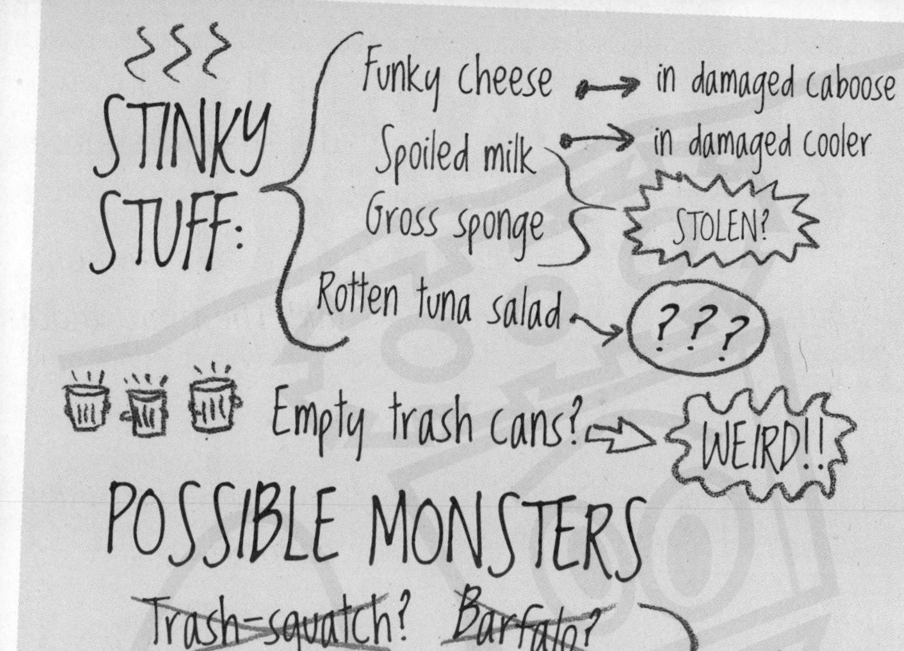

The caboose-crasher can't be a skunky-monkey, Alexander thought as he wadded up the scrap paper. *I really wish I had the notebook!*

CHAPTER

8 CLASH IN THE TRASH

KA-PLASH! A crashing sound woke Alexander in the middle of the night.

Is the neighbor's dog in our trash again? he thought.

Alexander grabbed a flashlight and threw on his rose-scented bathrobe. Then he tiptoed downstairs and out the front door.

He swung his flashlight around. The trash can was on its side. Even though the lid was shut, Alexander could smell the rotten-egg-and-tuna salad inside.

GRUNT-GRUNT-GRUNT!

It looked like a shaggy dog was sniffing around the can. No, wait. It had a pig's snout.

Then, with a snort, the creature . . . changed. A jagged saw-shaped thing popped out of the side of its head.

RINN-NIN-NN-NINNN-NIN!!

The blade sawed through the trash can. The yellow bowl rolled out, spilling tuna salad everywhere. The shaggy thing took a deep sniff, and purred.

A chill shot up Alexander's spine. He backed away from the creature, and — **ZWOOP!** — tripped on the front porch step.

Alexander's flashlight tumbled end-over-end, briefly throwing light into the monster's green eyes before hitting the ground and going dark.

Alexander felt around in the grass for his flashlight.

The monster reared up, dark against the moonlit fog. The saw-blade-thing was gone. Now the monster had a pointy gray horn.

A rhino horn! thought Alexander. *This monster is definitely the caboose-crasher!*

HOO-RONNNNNK!!!

The monster pawed at the ground. Then it lowered its horn and charged straight for Alexander.

Alexander shut his eyes and braced himself. But the crash never came.

SNORT! SNARF! ARF! The monster whimpered. Alexander could feel its breath as it sniffed his sleeve and chest.

Then it inhaled a long, raspy breath, and:

The monster sneezed all over Alexander, showering him in slime.

"Yeeearggggh!" Alexander jumped up, opening his eyes. He thought he'd be nose-to-nose with the monster. But it had run off, leaving behind a trail of snot.

CHAPTER

9 SMELLY CLUES

As Alexander arrived on the thirteenth floor the next morning, he saw Principal Vanderpants. She was carrying the white bucket. Clouds of steam were rising from it!

What could be in that bucket? he wondered.

He pretended to use the water fountain as he watched his principal. She set her bucket down near the UPSTAIRS BASEMENT door. Then she unlocked the stone door, and hauled the bucket inside.

Alexander speed-walked to the door and put his ear to it. The scratching sounds were louder than yesterday.

KER-CLICK! The door began to open.

Alexander dashed to Ms. Vanderpants's office and plopped in his seat.

A minute later, Ms. Vanderpants arrived. She put down the now-empty white bucket and stared at Alexander.

"Uh, good morning," said Alexander.

Ms. Vanderpants eyed Alexander. Then she dropped a thousand-page workbook on his desk. "Let's get to work, shall we?"

Alexander got to work.

Seventy-two pages later, the lunch bell rang. Alexander rushed downstairs.

"Over here, Salamander!" shouted Nikki. The S.S.M.P. waved him to their table.

“Guys! Guess what!” said Alexander. “I saw the caboose-crasher last night! It dug through my garbage and then charged right at me!”

Everyone gasped.

“How come there’s not a giant hole in your gut?” asked Rip.

“I’m not sure,” said Alexander. “The monster got close to me, but it sneezed and ran off. Here, I drew a sketch.”

“That thing sneezes?” said Rip. “So that puddle I fell in was actually . . . monster snot?!”

“Hey,” said Nikki. “There was snot all over our flower pots this morning!”

"And something dug up our compost heap," said Rip. "Moldy grapes, stale bread, wilted cabbage — all gone!"

"I'm not sure if it's connected," said Dottie. "But yesterday I swear I saw an elephant's trunk sticking out behind my fence. I ran to look, but it had disappeared!"

"Hmm . . ." said Alexander. "The monster I saw had a pig snout. And, like, a saw-blade-thing. And a rhino horn. But no trunk."

"I guess we should keep our, uh, noses open for anything stinky," said Nikki.

"In the meantime," said Alexander, "let's get ready for Dottie's birthday!"

"Yes!" said Dottie. "Soon, we'll be partying like pirates! Remember, I'll meet you at the golf course."

CHAPTER 10 PUTTER'S COVE

Alexander returned to the principal's office after lunch. There was a message on the board.

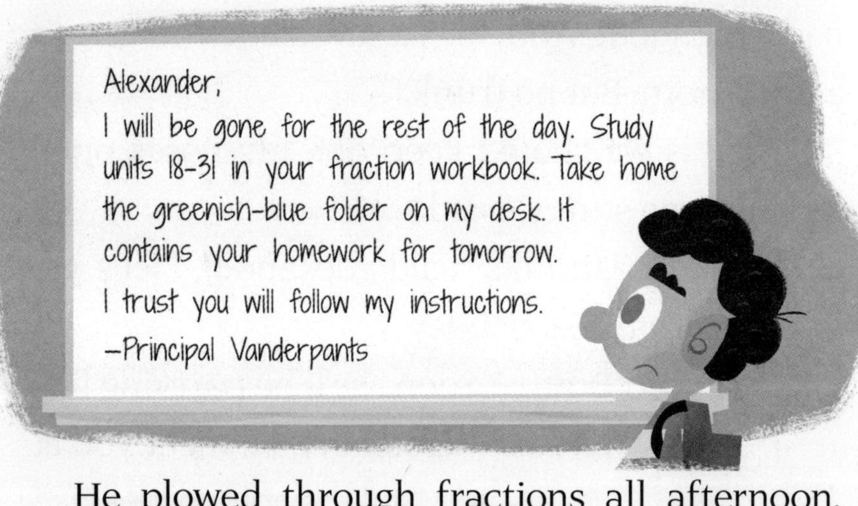

He plowed through fractions all afternoon. Finally, the last bell rang. He grabbed the bluish-green folder from Principal Vanderpants's desk and then raced downstairs. Rip and Nikki were waiting outside.

BEEP-BEEP! Alexander's dad pulled up. "Who's ready for mini-golf?"

"I can't wait to play," said Nikki.

"I can't wait to *win*!" said Rip.

The three friends piled into the backseat.

Soon, they pulled into Putter's Cove.

"Have fun, mateys," said Alexander's dad. "I'll pick you up later."

They hopped out of the car.

"This place sure looks piratey," said Nikki.

"It even *smells* piratey," said Rip, sticking out his tongue. "Like a bunch of sweaty, hairy guys on a boat."

Alexander held his nose. "I don't think Putter's Cove is *supposed* to smell like this," he said.

"No kidding," said a pirate lady, handing out scorecards.

"This lagoon started stinking a few days ago, and it keeps getting worse."

Rip turned over his scorecard. "Cool! There's a map on the back."

"The party room is in the lighthouse," said the pirate lady.

"Follow me!" said Rip.

The lighthouse was full of balloons, presents, and party guests. But no Dottie.

Alexander, Rip, and Nikki could see the whole golf course from here. Fake islands, a fake ship, and a fake volcano were all built on a large fake lagoon.

A wooden dam curved around one side, with a big treasure chest on top.

"Look! The smell must be coming from that gross water," said Nikki. She pointed to the murky gray lagoon surrounding the golf course.

Alexander checked his map.

PUTTER'S
COVE
1
2
3
4
5
THE OLD
WINDMILL
BOTTLE
BAY
LIGHTHOUSE
& PARTY ROOM
SEAHORSE
SHALLOWS
PARKING
18
CLAM'S
LANDING
17
SKELETON SHIP
QUICKSAND CAPE
16
BEACHED
WHALE

GLOAMY DAM
GLOAMY RIVER
6
SHARK FIN SHOAL
8
7
VOLCANO CAVE
SWIRLING WHIRLPOOL
9
JELLYFISH JETTY
IRON ANCHOR
10
14
11
MAD MERMAID
CORAL REEF
12
13
15
LOOKOUT SPIRE
PYTHON PIT
PELICAN POINT

"AHOY!"

A pirate with a silver golf-club sword and a tee-shaped peg leg strolled into the room.

"I be Cap'n Putterbeard!" he yelled. "And I welcome you — I mean *ye* — to Putter's Cove!"

The captain handed out putters to the guests.

"Hey, Putterbeard!" Rip yelled. "Why does this place stink like old gym socks?"

The captain pulled a parrot puppet from his sash and made it talk. "**AWK!** Sorry for the foul stench! We hope to have the course shipshape soon!"

"Thanks, Admiral Squawks!" said the captain. "Now, let's welcome our birthday girl: Dottie!"

Dottie entered the lighthouse. The party guests cheered.

"Hi, everyone!" said Dottie. She hopped over to Alexander, Rip, and Nikki. "The whole lagoon stinks," she whispered. "I think the monster —"

"BLARRRRRR!" Cap'n Putterbeard interrupted. "It's time ye be opening yer presents!"

"Yippee!" said Dottie.

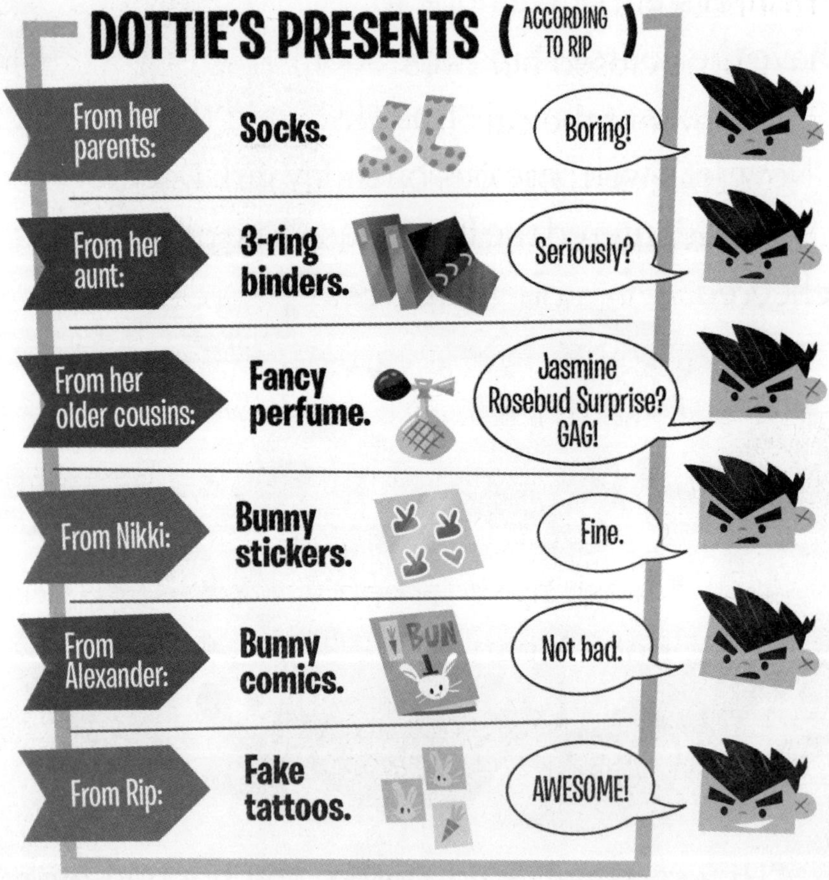

Dottie set her gifts on a large wooden barrel. "Thanks, everyone!" she said.

"AWK!" squawked Admiral Squawks. "Time for cupcakes!"

Cap'n Putterbeard held a birthday cupcake in front of Dottie.

Dottie closed her eyes and blew out the candle.

"THAR SHE BLOWS!" said the pirate.

Alexander noticed two things happen at once.

1. Dottie's eyes got a dreamy, faraway look.
2. **HOO-RONNNNNK!!!**

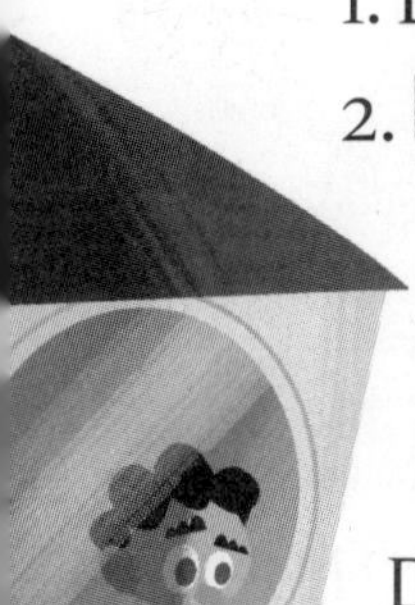

Alexander ran to the window and gasped. The monster was no longer crashing cabooses. Now it was crashing Dottie's party.

CHAPTER 11

NO TIME FOR TREATS

The shaggy, brown monster was sniffing the ground near a seahorse statue.

Alexander raced over to Nikki, Rip, and Dottie. "Guys!" he said. "The monster's here! We've got to get down there!"

"Hmmm?" said Dottie, looking up from her cupcake.

Rip ran to the window. "It just ducked into the windmill!"

Rip, Nikki, and Alexander started moving toward the door. But not Dottie.

"Aren't you coming?" asked Nikki, touching Dottie's shoulder.

Dottie blinked. "Huh?" she asked. "Don't leave yet — it's cupcake time!" She grabbed Rip's arm. "Here, Rip. Since you had that weird reaction to the strawberry cupcake, we made you a chocolate one!"

Rip looked at Alexander. Alexander shrugged back.

"Uh, okay. Thanks!" said Rip. He scarfed the cupcake down in two seconds.

"Why are you guys in such a rush?" asked Dottie. She handed cupcakes to Alexander and Nikki.

"You know why," said Alexander. He made claw-hands and said under his breath: "The monster, Dottie!"

"The lobster?" said Dottie.

"No!" said Rip, tossing his cupcake wrapper aside. "The *monster*! The one Salamander saw last night."

Dottie laughed. "There's no such thing as monsters! I love playing S.S.M.P. with you, but it's just a game — like with the knit-wit." She winked at Alexander. Then she passed out cupcakes to the rest of the guests.

Rip looked at Alexander and Nikki. "What's up with her?" he asked, scratching his ear.

CHAPTER 12 LOOK OUT BELOW

DING-DING-DING! Cap'n Putterbeard rang a bell mounted on the wall.

"Grab your putters, mateys! It's golf time!" he shouted. The partygoers followed him downstairs.

"So what's the plan, Salamander?" asked Nikki.

"I guess we pretend to play mini-golf while we search for the monster," said Alexander. "We'll start at the windmill —" He froze. "Rip, your ears are blue again!"

"Nuts!" said Rip. He clamped his hands over his ears.

"You must be allergic to *all* cupcakes," said Nikki. "You shouldn't have eaten the whole thing. Yesterday, you were splotchy from just one bite!"

"I'm sure I'll get better," he said. "Like yesterday."

The golfers split up. Alexander, Rip, and Nikki were grouped together, while Dottie played with her cousins.

Alexander's group ran from hole to hole, looking for clues. Rip saw something brown and shaggy in the cave at hole #7, but it was just a fake gorilla.

Nikki slipped on a snot-puddle near the anchor at hole #10.

"Looks like we're getting warmer!" she said.

". . . and stinkier," said Rip. "This lagoon is a dump!"

HOO-RONNNNNK!!!

"Another honk!" said Alexander.

Nikki checked the treasure map. "It came from the python pit at hole #12!"

"No way," said Rip, yanking the map away. "It came from that giant telescope at hole #13!"

"Incoming!" said a voice.

PLOP! A purple golf ball landed in the snot puddle.

"Oh, hey!" Dottie hopped across the bridge and picked up her ball. "Are you having fun?" she asked.

HOO-RONNNNNK!!!

The honk startled Alexander, Rip, and Nikki. But Dottie kept smiling.

"Didn't you hear that?" asked Rip.

"Hear what?" asked Dottie.

"The monster!" cried Alexander. He pointed to the treasure chest up on the dam.

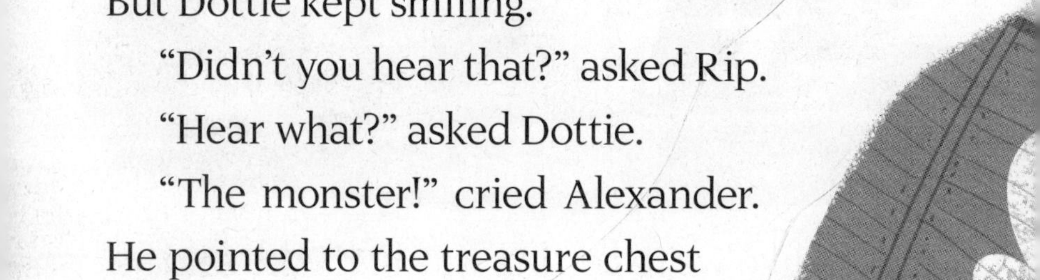

The huge, shaggy beast stood beside the chest. It had big round eyes, and a snout like a pig. It snorted angrily and — **FWOP!** — seven more noses popped out of its body.

CHAPTER 13

HARD TO SEE

Dottie looked where Alexander was pointing. "I see a treasure chest," she said.

"Look next to the chest," said Alexander.

"There's a giant *monster*, Dottie!" said Rip.

Dottie rolled her eyes. "Very funny," she said.

Alexander's jaw dropped. "You don't see it?"

"It has six . . . seven . . . eight noses!" said Rip. "Whoa! That's a lot of schnozzes!"

"It's an octo-schnozz!" said Nikki.

Dottie frowned. "Play 'monsters' if you want, but I've got a golf game to finish."

FWOP! The monster's noses disappeared into its shaggy fur. Except for the elephant trunk.

HOO-RONNNNNK!!!

The octo-schnozz dragged a dirty sack over to the chest.

"We're wasting time, guys!" said Rip. "Let's go!"

The S.S.M.P. watched Dottie trot off to play mini-golf with her cousins.

"Guys," said Alexander. "How could she not see —"

HRUNNK! With a grunt, the monster pulled some items from the sack and tossed them in the chest.

"My dad's tuna salad!" said Alexander.

"Mr. Hoarsely's grody, old sponge!" said Rip.

"The missing milk cartons!" said Nikki.

Alexander climbed up the anchor for a better look.

"The whole chest is full of garbage!" he said. "The schnozz has been stealing stinky stuff from all over town!"

"Is it eating the garbage?" asked Rip, scratching his ears.

"How? It doesn't have a mouth," said Nikki.

FWOP! The octo-schnozz's elephant trunk became a bloodhound snout. It took a long sniff of the smelly treasure, and made a purring sound.

"That thing loves bad smells!" said Alexander.

"I should give it my gym bag," Rip said.

"Um, Rip," said Nikki. "Not only are your ears blue — they look a little . . . pointy!"

"Huh?" Rip touched his ears.

"Are you sure you feel okay?" asked Alexander.

Rip stuffed his hands into his pockets. "Yes, weenie, I'm fine. Just —"

HOO-RONNNNNK!!!

CHAPTER

14 RUNNY NOSE

The octo-schnozz hopped down from the dam, landing in a cluster of palm trees. Alexander, Rip, and Nikki hid in a fake coral reef at hole #11.

The octo-schnozz snorfled its way to a trash can. Then — **FWOP!** — a sharp eagle's beak popped out. It snipped through the trash can. Garbage spilled onto the putting green.

"That's how it tore into the milk cooler!" Alexander whispered.

FWOP! The eagle beak became a pig snout. With a happy grunt, the monster rooted through the garbage.

FWOP! Out popped a seal nose.

The monster balanced the trash on its nose, and waddled over to the edge of the lagoon.

"It's tossing garbage into the water!" said Nikki.

The octo-schnozz looked out at the floating garbage and made an oinky-snort.

"It sounds . . . happy!" said Rip.

Then the monster looked across the bay, and stopped oinking. It was staring at a skeleton ship with a huge cannon. The monster began hopping and grunting.

"Why is it so worked up about that ship?" said Nikki.

Rip scratched his ears. "Cannons don't smell bad, do they?"

"Rip, your blue spots are back!" said Alexander. "Maybe we should —"

"Not now!" said Rip. "Let's go get this odor-eater!"

Alexander, Rip, and Nikki watched the octo-schnozz charge toward the ship. The monster trampled a field of tropical flowers, and began to whimper. It steered away from the flowers, and continued toward the ship.

Nikki snapped her fingers. "I have an idea!" She got to her feet. "I'll meet you on the ship!" Nikki turned and ran toward the lighthouse.

CHAPTER 15

SNOT A GOOD IDEA

Alexander and Rip had no trouble following the octo-schnozz, thanks to its excited grunts.

They followed the monster from the mermaid statue to the pelican roost to the beached whale. But the octo-schnozz was always one snort ahead of them.

Alexander and Rip chased the monster past Dottie and her cousins, but none of them seemed to see the monster. Nor did they seem to notice Rip's blue spots and pointy blue ears.

"We're closing in on it, Rip!" yelled Alexander.

Rip didn't say anything.

The octo-schnozz raced along the path. It gave a happy snort as it scampered aboard the skeleton ship.

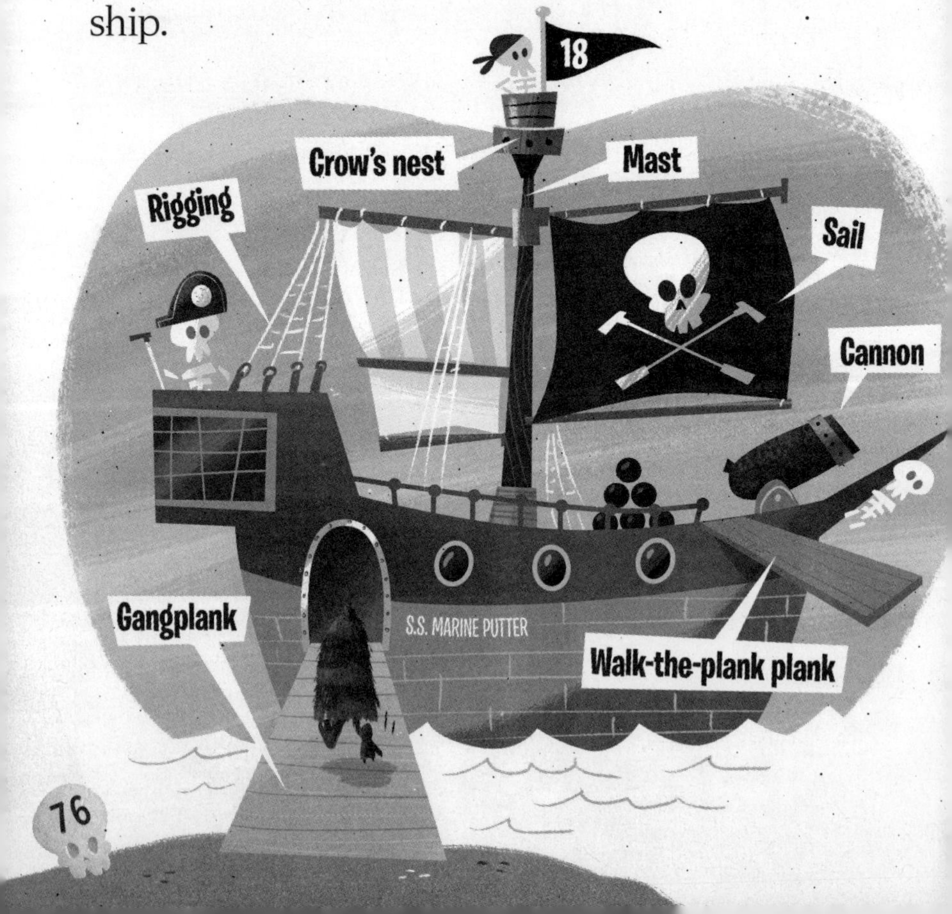

"Keep up, Rip!" said Alexander.

Alexander looked back. Rip was running strangely now, hunched over and dragging his knuckles on the ground. His blue spots were much bigger than yesterday.

"Oh no," said Alexander. "Here, Rip, rest on this bench. I'll deal with the monster until Nikki gets —"

HURN-HURN-HURN!!! The octo-schnozz turned and made laughing snorts at Alexander and Rip. Then it popped out its sawfish blade.

RINNN-NINNN-NINN-NNN!

The sharp blade tore through the gangplank, which fell aside in two pieces.

"*Now* how do we get onto the ship?" Alexander said.

The monster ran to the ship's rusty cannon. **FWOP!** It switched to a humongous human nose. It pressed one nostril shut with its elephant trunk and **BLOOMP!** It dropped a bowling-ball-size booger into the cannon's barrel.

"So gross," said Alexander.

The octo-schnozz pointed the cannon across the lagoon, directly toward the dam. The monster plugged its elephant trunk into the back of the cannon, and blew hard.

HOO-RONNNNNK!!!

The booger-bomb sailed over the lagoon.

BLAMMO! It slammed into the dam. A crack appeared, running all the way up the dam to the giant treasure chest on top. The chest tipped over, spilling two tons of garbage into the lagoon.

"Nooo!!" yelled Alexander.

The monster loaded another booger into the cannon.

"Rip, the octo-schnozz is going to destroy the dam!" Alexander said. "If that happens, this nasty water will flood the town! Who knows what kind of monsters that would attract?"

Rip didn't answer. Instead, he closed his eyes, arched his back, and roared.

Alexander gasped. His best friend was a monster.

CHAPTER 16 COMMON SCENTS

Monster-Rip leaped to the deck of the skeleton ship.

"Whoa!" said Alexander.

WHAM! Monster-Rip threw a monster-punch, knocking the octo-schnozz into the ship's mast.

The schnozz aimed its nostrils, and fired twin booger-blasts. **BLOOMP-BLOOMP!**

Monster-Rip batted the boogers away with his massive fists.

The monsters circled each other, growling.

"There are *two* monsters?!" shouted a voice.

Nikki was standing on a boulder, holding a rope connected to the ship's mast. She swung onto the ship's railing.

"Hey, where's Rip?" she asked.

"That blue monster *is* Rip!" Alexander yelled. "Now help me up!"

Nikki tossed down her rope, and Alexander climbed aboard.

The monsters let out a battle roar. Actually, one roared. **GRAAAWWRRR!!!** The other honked. **HOO-RONNNNNK!!!**

Then they lowered their horns and charged.

The pirate ship rocked from the monster-collision, sending waves across the lagoon.

The octo-schnozz staggered backward — **DING!** It hit its head against a bell, and fell to the deck.

Monster-Rip was dizzy, too. He stumbled sideways and slipped on a snot puddle.

Nikki and Alexander ran over. "Are you okay?" asked Nikki.

Rip shook his head a few times. He was back to normal.

"What . . . happened?" Rip said. "Did I just . . . ?"

". . . transform into a monster and knock out the octo-schnozz?" said Alexander. "Yup!"

"What the heck was in Dottie's cupcakes?!" Rip asked.

SNARF! The octo-schnozz hopped to its feet and staggered toward Rip.

"You leave Rip alone, schnozzy!" said Nikki, pulling a small bottle from her pocket. "Or I'll give you a whiff of Jasmine Rosebud Surprise!"

The monster stomped forward.

Nikki ran to the octo-schnozz, and aimed the bottle straight up its largest nostril. **PSSSHT-PSSSHT!** She sprayed a double pump of Dottie's birthday present.

The monster sniffled. Its eyes watered. It took a few loopy steps backward.

"The octo-schnozz's weakness is *flowers*!" said Nikki. "When it smelled the viney flowers on our caboose, and the field of tropical flowers —"

"And last night!" added Alexander. "It ran off when it smelled my flower-scented bathrobe!"

"Right!" said Nikki. "Flowery smells make the octo-schnozz have a big, fat —"

The monster inhaled, long and deep.

"AAH . . . AHHHH . . . AHHHHHHH . . ."

"Sneeze!" said Rip.

"Abandon ship!" shouted Alexander.

The S.S.M.P. dove overboard.

The octo-schnozz blasted a hurricane sneeze that filled the sails on the pirate ship.

The ship flew across the lagoon, propelled by the powerful sneeze. **CRRRUNCH!** It rammed into the volcano. A giant skull fell onto the ship, flattening the octo-schnozz!

The monster exploded like a hairy water balloon. Snot rained down on Putter's Cove, making all eighteen putting greens a bit greener.

Alexander, Nikki, and Rip swam ashore. They were tired, beat-up, wet, and stinky, but they were alive.

Across the harbor, they could see Dottie still golfing with her cousins.

“I guess this means the S.S.M.P. is back to three members, huh?” said Alexander.

“It sure looks that way,” Nikki agreed.

“And the boss-monster still has the notebook!” said Rip.

“We’ll get it back,” said Alexander. “For now, I’ll write up the octo-schnozz.”

He searched his backpack for a sheet of paper and pulled out the bluish-green folder. "Uh, guys," he said. "Take a look at this!"

"Those people were all monsters!" said Nikki.

"Monsters who attacked the S.S.M.P.!" said Rip.

"And three of them worked at our school — hired by Principal Vanderpants!" said Alexander. He swallowed. "Could this mean the boss-monster is —"

"Our principal!" cried all three friends at once.

Alexander's heart began to race as he quickly put the folder away.

Then he flipped over his treasure map, and scribbled some notes about the octo-schnozz.

OCTO-SCHNOZZ

An eight-nosed creature that's a total stinker.

SNORT! If an octo-schnozz laughs, will milk shoot out its nose?

DIET The octo-schnozz has no mouth. Maybe it survives on bad smells alone?

HABITAT Mini-golf course converted into a stink-pit!

BEHAVIOR This monster fires cannonball-sized boogers, and leaves a trail of slippery snot.

WARNING! Flowers make the octo-schnozz sneeze like a hurricane!

TROY CUMMINGS

has no tail, no wings, no fangs, no claws, and only one head. As a kid, he believed that monsters might really exist. Today, he's sure of it.

BEHAVIOR This creature's highly-trained schnozz can pick up the smell of sausage-onion pizza from three rooms away!

HABITAT Libraries and bookstores.

DIET Cinnamon toast. With extra butter. And extra cinnamon. And extra toast.

EVIDENCE Few people believe that Troy Cummings is real. The only proof we have is that he supposedly wrote and illustrated The Eensy-Weensy Spider Freaks Out!, and Giddy-up, Daddy!

WARNING Keep your eyes peeled for more danger in The Notebook of Doom #12:

MARCH OF THE VANDERPANTS